ELLA CARA DELORIA
Dakota Language Protector

DIANE WILSON

MINNESOTA NATIVE AMERICAN LIVES SERIES

ISBN 13: 978-1-63489-364-0
Library of Congress Catalog Number: 2020913755
Printed in the United States of America
First Printing: 2020

24 23 22 21 20   5 4 3 2 1

Illustrations © 2020 Tashia Hart
Book design by Patrick Maloney

This work is funded with money from the Arts and Cultural Heritage Fund that was created with the vote of the people of Minnesota on November 4, 2008.

Minnesota
Humanities
Center

Wise Ink Creative Publishing
807 Broadway St. NE, Suite 46
Minneapolis, MN 55413
wiseink.com

To order, visit itascabooks.com or call 1-800-901-3480. Reseller discounts available.

CONTENTS

Introduction   1

1. The Dakota Way of Life   3

2. Learning New Ways   9

3. Living in Two Cultures   15

4. Becoming a Storyteller   22

5. Staying True to Herself   26

6. A Good Relative   33

Ideas for Writing and Discussion   39

Ideas for Visual Projects   40

Ideas for Further Learning   42

Timeline   45

About the Author   49

About the Illustrator   50

About the Series Editors   51

INTRODUCTION

S torytelling is a traditional tool of many Indigenous people, and here in Minnesota our storytelling tradition is alive and well among Native Americans of many nations. The authors, illustrators, and editors of this series, who are all Dakota or Ojibwe, continue their cultural traditions in creating these books.

The Minnesota Humanities Center and the editors of this series of books for younger readers believe it is important to envision the future through stories of the past and present. Our goal is to help Native American children see their cultures represented alongside biographies of other leaders in our larger society. We envisioned a series of children's books by, for, and about Dakota and Anishinaabe (Ojibwe) and other Indigenous people, portraying our histories, knowledge ways, culture keepers, and beloved figures. These biographies are meant to help Dakota, Anishinaabe, and other Native American children imagine their own potential for full futures.

Of all the children's books published in the United States, only 1 percent are written by Native and First Nations authors, according to the Cooperative Children's Book Center at the University of Wisconsin–Madison.[1]

Our hope is that teachers and parents will encourage young readers

---

1 Data on books by and about people from First/Native Nations published for children and teens compiled by the Cooperative Children's Book Center, School of Education, University of Wisconsin–Madison. ccbc.education.wisc.edu/books/pcstats.asp

to see themselves in the extraordinary lives presented in these stories. We also hope readers will consider how the facts of social barriers based in race, culture, education, and class influenced the lives of the subjects of these books. History, especially the impacts of treaties, underlies these stories as well. These are narratives that open up contexts of language and culture and the policies meant to destroy them. The legacy of boarding schools and forced education away from family figures into each story to some extent. Poverty and the disruption of family life are also themes too many children can relate to, and the women and men featured in these narratives overcame just such circumstances.

The first books in this series include stories of historic figures who lived, worked, and broke barriers a hundred years ago, as well as the ongoing story of an exceptional Ojibwe woman who rose to the highest levels of leadership in Minnesota and in the nation.

—Gwen Nell Westerman and Heid E. Erdrich,
series editors, May 2020

Chapter One

THE DAKOTA WAY OF LIFE

"The ultimate aim of Dakota life, stripped of accessories, was quite simple: One must obey kinship rules; one must be a good relative."

—Ella Cara Deloria, *Speaking of Indians*

When Ella was a young girl, she lived on the Standing Rock Reservation in South Dakota. She was a good student who loved to read. She especially enjoyed visiting with the grandfathers and grandmothers who lived nearby.

With her warm smile and good manners, Ella would have been a welcomed guest. She listened closely to them and learned to speak Lakota. Even as a child, Ella had a gift for languages.

Today, Ella is well-known for helping to save the language and culture of her Dakota people. Through her work, she recorded important Dakota stories so future generations would know them too.

Long before Ella was born, the Dakota homeland sprawled across what is now North and South Dakota, Minnesota, Iowa, Nebraska, Wyoming, Montana, and parts of Canada. Although traders and explorers called them "Sioux," their true name is Dakota, which means "friendly" or "ally."

The Dakota people are made up of three groups who live in different regions and speak different versions of the Dakota language. The Santee or Eastern Dakota speak the Dakota dialect and they live near the lakes and woods along the Minnesota River and Red

3

River. The Yankton or Central Dakota speak Dakota or Nakota and live on the prairies. And the Teton or Western Dakota, who live on the plains, speak Lakota. These groups of Dakota people are also called the Oceti Sakowiŋ, or Seven Council Fires.

Ella's grandfather, Saswe, was born in 1816. Back then, the Dakota people moved from camp to camp as they followed the bison. This large animal is sometimes called buffalo. Millions of bison roamed the plains, some weighing up to two thousand pounds. When they stampeded across the land, it sounded like thunder.

The Dakota families honored the buffalo as a relative who gave its life so they could survive. Their hides were used to make tipis, blankets, and winter coats. A single buffalo provided many pounds of meat that could be roasted or dried for winter. Their bones were made into tools such as needles and garden hoes. Their ribs were made into sleds for children to play with. Nothing was wasted. Today, many Dakota tribes have bison herds on their reservations.

Through the long winters, the people watched groups of stars move across the sky. As these constellations changed, they knew the right time to move to their summer camps. The Seven Sisters constellation showed them when it was time to plant their corn and squash. Astronomers also call this constellation the Pleiades.

During this time, the Dakota did not need books or a written language. Instead, they saved their history by telling oral stories. Each year, or winter, had a name and a story about a memorable event that happened. These stories, called winter counts, were repeated many times so they would not be forgotten.

Remembering so many stories is not easy. A good storyteller is like an actor who can make people laugh or cry. In Saswe's time, some storytellers could remember three hundred winter counts! A

family might offer a feast and gifts to a storyteller who shares these stories with the children. The ohuŋkaŋkaŋ are very old stories about spirit beings, like the trickster Iktomi. Others are about family life and how things came to be on this earth.

Grandparents also tell stories to help their grandchildren learn to behave. They don't like to yell or get mad. When Iktomi gets in trouble in a story, a grandmother might say, "He is very bad, that Iktomi. He does things that are not done. He is not a real human being." That way, children learn not to behave like Iktomi.

Ella's grandfather, Saswe, was raised this way as a Dakota boy. Almost as soon as he could talk, he learned kinship terms. These terms are a polite way of speaking to each family member instead of calling them by their names. Saswe called his father Até and his mother Ina. Saswe knew his father's brother would be like another father, and his mother's sister would be like another mother. Saswe's uncles and aunts helped him through his life. The Dakota people lived closely together in camps and these kinship rules helped everyone get along and know their families. These rules are very important to the Dakota way of life.

Dakota children grew up in a large family, surrounded by aunts, uncles, grandparents, grandchildren, and cousins. This extended family, or tiośpaye, helped raise each child by teaching them skills and kinship rules. The men taught young boys how to ride horses, hunt and fish, and fight when necessary. Young girls learned from their mothers and aunts to care for the home and garden, gather plants, and raise children. Girls and boys were equally important to their community. Everyone learned the stories and rules, and everyone had a role in their community.

When Saswe was a young man, he had a vision. In his dream,

he had to choose which road to follow. The left side showed four generations who would prosper but give nothing to the world. The right side, or red road, would be dangerous but filled with great opportunities. Saswe chose the red road. He was shown how to use plant medicines and become a healer for his people.

Saswe's vision was so powerful that he saw his life in a new way. He knew the world was changing and his family would have to change with it.

Chapter Two

LEARNING NEW WAYS

"It came and without their asking for it—a totally different way of life, far reaching in its influence, awful in its power, insistent in its demands. It came like a flood that nothing could stay."

—Ella Cara Deloria, *Speaking of Indians*

By 1850, the trickle of immigrants moving into Dakota homeland had become a flood of people. They brought new ideas and a hunger for land that threatened the Dakota way of life. Hunters slaughtered millions of bison for sport until the bison were nearly extinct. Unlike Dakota hunters, these people killed for hides and trophies, and left the meat to rot. Without the bison, Dakota families would not have enough food.

The United States government made treaties with the Dakota people, who agreed to give up some of their land in exchange for promises of food and payments. The treaties set aside areas of land called reservations. Instead of moving freely throughout their homeland, the Dakota were supposed to live only on these new reservations.

But the government wanted more than land. They also wanted to "civilize" the Dakota people by persuading them to live in houses like Americans and learn to farm. Many churches sent missionaries to teach them to become Christians. The missionaries did not understand that these Dakota men and women were already spiritual

people with their own beliefs. They did not want to change how they had lived for many generations.

Saswe wanted to help his people learn to live in this changing world. In 1873, he chose to be baptized as a Christian by the Episcopal Church. They gave him a new name: Francis Deloria. His family began to follow both traditional Dakota and Christian beliefs. Saswe's son, Tipi Sapa, had grown up helping him gather plants for medicine to help their Dakota relatives. Now, living on a reservation, he had to find another way to serve his people.

Tipi Sapa was seventeen when he was invited to live at the Episcopal Mission on the Yankton Reservation. Tipi Sapa was asked repeatedly to cut his hair, dress like an American, and go to school. Each time he said no. Finally, after many talks with the minister and his father, he agreed. Tipi Sapa believed this was the best way he could help his people, but it also meant he had to face their disapproval.

"Coward. He fears warfare," they said. "See, he chooses an easy life."

It was not easy to hear these insults. He decided to change his name. From then on, Tipi Sapa was called Philip Deloria.

After attending college for two years, Philip returned to his reservation in 1874. He worked at churches in different communities. In 1885, he was sent to the Standing Rock Reservation to take charge of St. Elizabeth's Church. Sometimes he wrote his sermon by spending Saturday afternoons lying on the ground, watching clouds. He hoped studying the clouds would help him shape his thoughts into powerful words. Philip believed the Dakota should give up their traditional ways and join the church.

At Standing Rock, Philip met Akicita Wiŋ, whose English name was Mary Sully Bordeaux. Philip and Mary were married in 1888. Her father was Alfred Sully, a general in the US Army. Mary's mother, Pehaŋdutawiŋ, raised her as a traditional Dakota girl on the Yankton Reservation.

Ella was born in 1889, as strong blizzard winds blew heavy snow across the Yankton Reservation. Her mother had come home to give birth. Her father stayed behind on the Standing Rock Reservation for his job at St. Elizabeth's Church. Her parents named her Aŋpetu Wašté Wiŋ, Beautiful Day Woman, making a joke about the weather.

She was joined by her sister, Susan, in 1896. Susan would grow up to become a talented artist like her great-grandfather, Thomas Sully. In 1901, Ella's brother, Vine, was born. He would become a well-known priest, like his father. The Deloria children grew up speaking Dakota as their first language at home.

Many years later, Ella wrote a letter to her friend Margaret Mead. She described how she grew up so Margaret would understand her family. "My father and mother," she wrote, "were related to everyone, in social kinship. And so I was related to everyone too; and I always knew what kinship obligations were required of me."

Not far from the church, Philip helped start the St. Elizabeth's Mission School to teach Dakota children. The federal government and churches were setting up hundreds of boarding and mission schools across the country. Native children were required to attend school, or else their families would not be given the food they were promised. Sometimes children were taken away from their families and sent to school.

In the early days of the St. Elizabeth's school, only a few children

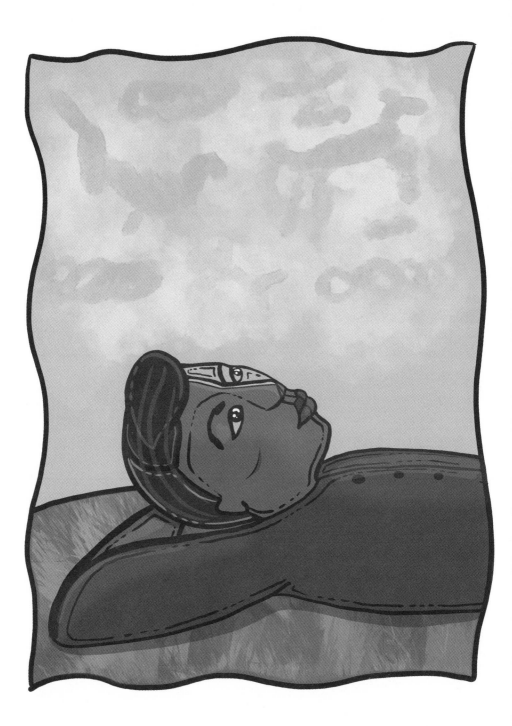

came. Many of the Dakota families did not want to change their way of life to become Christians. In just thirty years, the proud, independent Dakota people had been forced to give up much of their homeland. No longer able to hunt for themselves, they now had to rely on food from the government. They were angry at being cheated and afraid of losing their way of life.

Like her father, Ella would need to find a new way to help her people.

Chapter Three

LIVING IN TWO CULTURES

"But they were a people used to accepting fate with
fortitude and dignity."

—Ella Cara Deloria, *Speaking of Indians*

Just as Saswe had foreseen, learning this different way of life helped
the Deloria family survive. It also meant that Ella grew up in two
cultures.

Ella lived with her family in a big white house on a hill, not far
from the Episcopal church and St. Elizabeth's school. Below the hill,
Dakota families often camped in tipis for several days. They came to
visit with other families, pick up their food, and go to church.

Even as a child, Ella was fascinated by the stories she heard from
her family. Her father and his friends enjoyed sharing stories of the
past. When her parents traveled for church business, Ella's grandmother would set up her tipi in their yard. She often told stories
while caring for the children. Ella's mother and aunts also shared
stories about the Dakota way of life with her.

Sometimes Ella would sneak away to the nearby camp to listen
to the storytellers. Her family would find her sitting at a campfire,
her moccasins tucked beneath her long cotton dress. As an adult,
Ella remembered, "I kept my eyes and ears open and remember
pretty much all I ever saw and heard of Teton life in the past."

Ella was baptized as a Christian and spoke English at school.
She was expected to act differently there than she would at home.

When she was older, Ella wrote that this was a confusing way to grow up. "From a thorough Indian life," she said, "we were plunged into the cultured atmosphere at school, and then thrust back again each vacation. . . . It was a hard thing to go through."

Life at school was demanding. Students learned to read and write English, take care of the animals, cut hay, and chop wood. The girls helped cook and do the washing in big tubs. They also worked in the garden, growing vegetables for the kitchen. They went to the nearby rivers and hauled water in barrels back to the school. They used kerosene lamps and traveled by horse or wagon.

The older girls, like Ella, helped the young ones learn English. One little boy named Frank had a hard time learning to say the Lord's Prayer in English. While practicing with Ella, he sometimes slipped back into Lakota. She wanted to laugh, but she stopped herself so he could finish. Even though she was just a young girl, she was careful not to ridicule this little boy. Instead, she treated him with kindness so he would keep practicing English. Ella was already learning to become a teacher and mentor like her teacher Miss Francis.

At St. Elizabeth's school, Miss Mary Francis encouraged Ella's lifelong love of reading and learning. Miss Mary had lived in Dakota country since 1880. When she left their school in 1907, a big crowd came to see her off. When she died years later, Ella called her "a friend of the Dakota people."

Ella excelled as a student, but she always cared about the feelings of those around her. "I soon realized in that mission school that it was improper to be too smart," she said. "So even when I knew the answers, which was almost always except in arithmetic, I knew enough to keep still unless pressed." Having learned that lesson,

Ella soon had many friends. She loved to laugh and tell stories with the other girls.

When Ella was twelve, she was strong enough to drive a team of horses pulling a wagon. Once, while she was helping her father, something spooked the horses. They took off running! The wagon tipped, throwing Ella to the ground. She hurt her right thumb and it had to be removed. This accident made typing difficult for the rest of her life, but Ella did not let it slow her down. She was always an active girl, playing games, dancing, and helping with chores.

One morning while sitting in a pew at her father's church, Ella fell asleep. She dreamed that she was both a boy and a girl. She took money from her father and went off to another land, met other people, and came back home. At the end of the dream, Ella crossed back to the side of a river that was home. Her father forgave her for taking the money and her family welcomed her back. Over the years, she often thought about the meaning of this dream. It seemed to be telling her about the work she was supposed to do.

Ella left St. Elizabeth's when she was fourteen to go to the All Saints School in Sioux Falls, South Dakota. As the daughter of an underpaid minister, Ella was given a free high school education. This was Ella's first time living away from home. She was excited and nervous to be so far away from her family. Most of the students at this all-girls school were from successful American families. Ella's cheerful personality helped her make friends. She continued to do well in her classes, especially in English and Latin.

In her fourth and last year at All Saints, she wrote an essay that won her a scholarship to attend Oberlin College in Ohio. This was a big step for Ella. In 1910, she was one of the few Dakota women to go to college. Many young people from reservations were living at boarding schools, where they were not treated well. But Ella was ready for this opportunity. She was twenty-one, a hard worker, and hungry to learn.

Ella did so well at Oberlin that she transferred to the Teacher's College at Columbia University in New York. She and her sister, Susan, traveled there together. With so many tall buildings, the city was unlike anything they had ever seen before. Ella said New York was a place of "endless cement," where she did not feel connected to the earth. But the university offered new ways for Ella to keep learning.

Ella met Dr. Franz Boas, a well-known professor at Columbia University. He taught anthropology, the study of human beings. She did not know meeting Dr. Boas would change her life. He hired Ella to help his students learn the Lakota language and she earned her very first paycheck. She was paid $18 a month, which is about $460 today.

Ella enjoyed studying at Columbia University, but she realized many people knew little about her Dakota relatives. Some scholars had written articles about Dakota life that were not correct. Ella worried these mistakes would create more wrong ideas and harmful government policies. Life was already hard for the Dakota people. At that time, there were very few Dakota scholars who could defend the true story about their own people. Ella wondered if she could help by sharing what she knew about Dakota culture.

When Ella graduated in 1915, Native people were not American citizens, nor were they allowed to vote. Their spiritual practices were illegal. Ella was living in a world that treated Native people as inferior to other Americans. Women, both Dakota and American, were not allowed to vote.

Ella's first job was teaching back at her old school, All Saints. When Susan graduated from there in 1916, the two young women immediately went home to care for their sick mother. She died a short time later, and Ella knew she needed to help her family. She took care of her younger siblings and helped her father with his church work. She also needed to find a way to earn money to support them.

In 1918, with her younger brother, Vine, away at school, Ella returned with Susan to New York. She worked as the secretary of the YWCA, traveling to reservation schools around the country. The Haskell Institute in Lawrence, Kansas, hired her in 1923 to teach physical education to Native girls. She coached sports, taught dancing, and served as a substitute teacher. One of the students said Ella was someone who "always had a happy attitude." Another student was inspired by Ella to spend her life teaching Native children in boarding schools.

Unlike her father, Ella did not believe Dakota people had to give up who they were to be Americans. She gave a speech to students at St. Mary's Indian School for Girls in Springfield, South Dakota, where she taught occasionally. Ella encouraged them to learn to live with both cultures. "Success comes from endurance and persistence," she said. She repeated this message throughout her life.

To help the other teachers understand more about Dakota people, Ella wrote and produced two pageants. These all-day celebrations included ceremonials, games, dances, and songs. Ella discovered she had a talent for writing.

While Ella was at the Haskell Institute, she received a letter from a woman who was working with Dr. Boas. He remembered when Ella taught his students about the Lakota language. He wanted to know if she would help him with a translation project. Ella had enjoyed the work and agreed to help him.

Finally, twelve years after graduating from college, Ella was about to begin the work she cared about most.

Chapter Four

BECOMING A STORYTELLER

"I am very thoroughly convinced that you cannot really get at the heart of a people without knowing their language."

—Ella Cara Deloria, *Dakota Texts*

As Ella's life was about to change, the federal government was changing the way it treated Native people. A report showed that many people on reservations were poor. Boarding schools were a disaster. Children came home as strangers who did not belong in their communities. The tiospaye and kinship system were falling apart. The Dakota way of life was in danger of disappearing.

Living on her reservation, Ella saw the harm that was done through these schools. Fewer children were raised to speak their language. As grandparents died, so did the stories and traditions they knew. Students were forbidden to speak their language in schools, so there were no new speakers to take their place.

Ella knew that if Dakota families lost their language and stories, they would lose the heart of their culture. How would the Dakota people remember who they were?

In 1928, Ella returned to New York to begin working with Dr. Boas. Susan traveled with her. Susan's ill health meant she was not able to live on her own. She became Ella's companion and drove her wherever she needed to go. Susan was also a talented artist who worked with Ella on many projects. Using the name Mary Sully, she created hundreds of colored-pencil drawings about famous people. She called these drawings "Personality Prints."

Dr. Boas wanted Ella to help him translate many pages of Lakota stories into English. These stories had been collected in 1887 by George Bushotter, a Teton Dakota, for the Smithsonian Museum. Over time, Boas trained Ella to use scientific methods for recording language and stories. She learned to keep detailed records.

With his mentorship, Ella became one of the first Native ethnologists in the country. As an ethnologist, she studied the language and culture of the Dakota people. Finally, she knew the meaning of her dream. Ella had found a way to help her people.

She said she wanted to "study everything possible of Dakota life, and see what made it go, in the old days, and what was still so deeply rooted that it could not be rudely displaced without some hurt." Through her work, Ella learned the skills she needed to help preserve the Dakota language and culture.

Over the next fifteen years, Ella worked with Dr. Boas as his research assistant. She also translated Lakota and Dakota texts into English. She became friends with other women who had studied with Dr. Boas. One of them, Dr. Margaret Mead, became a famous anthropologist. Another well-known anthropologist, Dr. Ruth Benedict, helped Ella with her research and writing.

Ella often traveled between New York and South Dakota. Living in the city showed her a fast-paced new world. But South Dakota was always her home. She missed her family and her many Dakota friends. She enjoyed the work, but struggled to support herself and her family. Dr. Boas helped raise funds to pay her.

After Ella finished translating the Bushotter stories, she worked on the manuscripts of George Sword, a Teton Dakota, and Jack

Frazier, a Santee Dakota. She wrote papers that gave true information about Dakota culture. Ella and Boas together wrote an article on language that was published in 1933. Ella was beginning to get national recognition for her work as a linguist and ethnologist.

As Ella was becoming well known, she never changed the way she treated people. She cared about everyone she met. Many people called her Aunt Ella and described her as charming and kind. Throughout her life, Ella always tried to be a good relative.

She often gave speeches to groups who enjoyed her lively stories about Dakota life. Like her brother, Vine, she was a gifted speaker. Her stories showed how kinship rules had worked in her community. She shared her passion for the language by explaining the meaning of certain words. "There's so much left to tell," she said to one group. "So invite me back next year, and I'll tell you more!" Ella entertained her audience while making sure they learned true information about the Dakota.

Throughout her life, she thought the teachers and preachers who came to the reservations assumed "the Dakotas had nothing, no rules of life, no social organization, no ideals." And she knew that was not true. The work she was now doing made her happy. "I actually feel that I have a mission," she said, "to make the Dakota people understandable, as human beings, to the white people who have to deal with them."

One of the projects Ella cared about was recording stories from Teton Dakota communities. Over several years, she traveled across reservations looking for the oldest and most knowledgeable storytellers. She was searching for people who remembered the ohuŋkaŋkaŋ, the stories she heard as a child. Ella described these stories as "tales which are best known, oftenest repeated."

Rather than taking notes, Ella listened carefully and wrote them down later. Like a good storyteller, she needed a well-trained memory to do this work. Other times, she typed them on her typewriter as they were told to her. Her method was to write the story down "in the original, directly from storytellers who related them to me." Then she translated the story into English, just as it was said in Dakota. Finally, she wrote another version of the story so the meaning was the same in English.

Sixty-four of these stories were published as *Dakota Texts* in 1932. Ella's book is now considered to be one of the most important books written about the oral stories of the Teton Dakota. If Ella had not recorded these stories, they might have been lost as the storytellers passed away. Ella's one regret was not having enough money to publish more of the stories she collected.

In 1934, Congress passed the Indian Reorganization Act. The government realized its policies had not helped Native people. The act made many changes that were supposed to make life better. Sweeping reforms in boarding schools, for example, made them less harsh for children.

The world was very different from the one Ella had known as a child. She wanted more than ever to save the language and stories that were disappearing.

Chapter Five

STAYING TRUE TO HERSELF

"All human beings learn from each other. . . . The Indians, belonging to the great human family, have the same innate powers, inborn intelligence, and potentialities as the rest of mankind."

—Ella Cara Deloria, *Speaking of Indians*

Just as Ella's career was going well, her family had more money trouble. Dr. Boas could not always find funding for her work. Ella's father was ill. Her brother, Vine, was just entering the ministry. He was paid half as much as the white priests and could not help care for their father.

Ella often talked about money with Dr. Boas. She did not think it was fair for her to be paid less than white researchers.

Dr. Boas did not always understand the challenges Ella faced in her life. "I live in my car," she wrote to him. "All our things are in it. And if I go anywhere, I find it cheapest to go in my car, and take my sister with me. I love her. I cannot do otherwise than give her a home of sorts." Even with his help, she often did not have enough money to support her family.

True to her Dakota teachings, Ella did not care about owning things. She and her sister, Susan, often traveled in an old or borrowed car with her typewriter in the trunk. Sometimes she rented

a hotel room or stayed with Vine. Without a place of her own, her files were sometimes lost or damaged. Still, she took notes anytime she met Dakota people who were willing to share their stories. Over the years, she gathered the largest collection of stories of any tribe.

No matter how hard her life became, Ella's love of family was at the heart of her work. She never regarded them as a burden. To her, family was most important. She cared for her father throughout his long illness. Before he died in 1931, he often shared stories with her. He taught her about continuing the Dakota way of life, such as bringing food and gifts to the people she interviewed.

Ella firmly believed being a Dakota woman was helpful for her research. She knew how to ask people for their help. They trusted her to be careful with their information. Ella tried to explain to Boas why this was important. "If I go, bearing a gift, and gladden the hearts of the informants, and eat with them, and call them by the correct social kinship terms, then later I can go back, and ask them all sorts of questions, and get my information, as one would get favors from a relative," she wrote. "It is hard to explain, but it is the only way I can work."

In the academic world, some scholars did not like Ella because she was a Native woman. They said she couldn't be fair when studying Native people. When she found mistakes in the earlier work of white scholars, they ignored her. They said she wasn't well trained because she didn't have a degree in anthropology. Some people said she was a "loose cannon," a person whose work could not be trusted.

While Dr. Boas was a trusted mentor to Ella, even he did not always believe in her work. Once, he asked Ella to help verify or prove the work of Dr. James Walker. Dr. Walker was a physician who lived on

28

the Pine Ridge Reservation between 1896 and 1914. He collected many stories about Teton Dakota life. While the people Dr. Walker talked to were gone, Ella found one of their friends. She wrote to Dr. Boas that she was skeptical of Dr. Walker's information.

Boas wrote back that he was "not quite satisfied" with her comments. He asked her to do more research. She told him she could not find proof if it did not exist. By refusing to change her work, Ella maintained her integrity. Today, Dr. Walker's work is well-known, while much of Ella's work remains unpublished. She was ahead of her time in the way she thought about culture and anthropology. Only in more recent years has her work begun to receive the attention it deserves.

Despite their disagreement, Ella respected Dr. Boas and cared for him as a friend. Together, they published *Dakota Grammar* in 1941. On his eighty-first birthday, Ella wrote, "I would not trade the privilege of having known you for anything I can think of."

Ella found new ways to use her skills by helping other Native communities. In 1940, she was asked by the Bureau of Indian Affairs to study the Lumbee Indians in Pembroke, North Carolina. They had lost most of their history and language. Ella and Susan produced two pageants for the Lumbee about their early days as a tribe. Susan created artwork and painted the sets.

The Lumbee women told Ella the names of plants and animals, the food they cooked, and the folk medicines they used. She collected over three hundred words and phrases on little cards. She kept her notes in big traveling trunks in a rented storage place in Fort Lee, Virginia. Ella believed that with more time she could reconstruct their original language. This would have been a precious gift to the Lumbee people.

Sadly, Ella did not have enough money to pay for storing her trunks. Before she could complete the research, her trunks were sold to pay her overdue bill. Ella's work on the Lumbee language was lost. Her efforts to help the Lumbee reclaim their language and identity were never completed.

For many years, Ella kept a scrapbook that included newspaper articles, pageant programs, a poem by Elias Lieberman, and a recipe. Several of the articles were about the death of Dr. Boas in 1942. Ella lost a good friend and mentor when he died.

In her scrapbook, Ella also taped an article about her 1943 Indian Achievement Award from the Indian Council Fire in Chicago. This was the most important award a Native person could receive. In the newspaper photo, Ella's face is glowing with a happy smile. She was now recognized for her knowledge of Dakota language and culture. The award showed how much her work was appreciated by other Native people.

During World War II, Ella published her new book, *Speaking of Indians*. She wrote about Dakota people for white, Christian readers. She explained kinship rules and the importance of not caring too much about owning things. "If you wished to honor me publicly, you did not load me down personally with presents," she wrote. "You made someone else glad in my name." Ella dedicated *Speaking of Indians* to the memory of her beloved teacher, Miss Mary.

In her own life, Ella lived according to this teaching. She never stopped working or trying to make life better for her family and her people.

Chapter Six

A GOOD RELATIVE

"Not only what a people do, but how they *think* and *feel* to make them do it, are important to an understanding of their culture as a whole."

—Ella Cara Deloria,
American Philosophical Society Yearbook

As a scholar who also loved writing, Ella sometimes got tired of scientific rules. There was so much more she wanted to say about Dakota people. She wanted to show how kinship worked in daily life. She especially wanted to write about the traditional roles of Dakota women.

Before Ella, most of the histories about Dakota people had been written by white men. They rarely wrote about the role Dakota women played in their communities. Native women have always served their people as leaders, healers, and storytellers. When Europeans came, Native women were nearly erased from history. These men often believed women's work was less important than men's work.

As a Dakota woman, Ella knew women taught language and culture to their children. The Dakota people survived because women passed this knowledge to the next generation. Women were honored for the important roles they held in the tiospaye.

The study of anthropology began to change. Anthropologists realized people might learn more about other cultures by reading stories or novels instead of academic papers. Zora Neale Hurston was also Dr. Boas's student. She wrote about African American cultures and became a well-known novelist. Another of his students, Dr. Ruth Benedict, published poetry under another name. Ella knew these women from her time at Columbia University.

In 1942, Ella began working on her own novel, *Waterlily*. She wanted to tell the story of Dakota people from a woman's point of view. Using her years of research, Ella knew how to recreate life in the camp circle before the Europeans came. She wrote to her friend Dr. Margaret Mead that she hoped the novel would appeal to many readers. "Only my characters are imaginary," she said. "And it is purely the woman's point of view, her problems, aspirations."

The story opens as Blue Bird is about to give birth to her daughter, Waterlily. Their tiośpaye is moving to a new camp. Waterlily is raised as a traditional Dakota girl. As she grows up, Waterlily describes how they live, what they eat, and what they believe. Kinship rules are shown in the way the characters treat each other.

Waterlily's story showed how women shared knowledge with their children. By writing this novel, Ella gave Dakota women the respect they deserved. As a writer, she honored her own heart.

Ella worked on the novel for two years. Her friend Dr. Ruth Benedict helped edit *Waterlily*. By 1948, shortly before Ruth's death, the manuscript was ready to publish. Ella submitted the book to several publishers, all of whom turned it down. They said people were no longer interested in reading about Dakota life.

Waterlily was not published until 1988. Since then, *Waterlily* has become a treasured book that shows the beautiful life Dakota people had created. Her book helps people today learn about Dakota culture.

After finishing *Waterlily*, Ella had to find new ways to support herself and Susan. More than anything, Ella wanted to keep writing and collecting stories from Dakota people. She raised enough funds to work on a new manuscript, *Dakota Family Life: Social Patterns and Education*. This book shared more of her research on kinship and family life.

In 1955, Ella and Susan were hired to run St. Elizabeth's, the school they had attended as young girls. Then the University of South Dakota hired Ella in 1961 to be the assistant director of the W. H. Over Museum. Her job was to study Dakota language. With the support of a grant, Ella also worked on a Dakota dictionary.

Ella's sister and lifelong companion Susan passed away in 1963. Ella was sad to lose her sister after so many years together. But she was determined to keep working. Already in her seventies, Ella learned to drive so she could interview elders at remote reservations.

She kept on working until she became ill from a stroke. Ella died in 1971, in Wagner, South Dakota, not far from where she was born. She was buried at St. Philip's Church along with her sister, mother, grandmother, and other relatives. Her nephew, Vine Deloria Jr., said, "In death as in life, Ella was surrounded by family."

In all the ways that matter most, Ella Cara Deloria lived a good life. As a Dakota woman, she followed the kinship rules and cultural values that were so important to her. Through all the challenges she faced, Ella kept writing, recording stories, and taking care of her family.

After forty years, while typing with only nine fingers, Ella wrote sixteen different publications. She created several pageants that performed Native stories. Writing about kinship and women's roles became one of her most important contributions to the study of Dakota culture. Dr. Margaret Mead called Ella "an extraordinarily gifted person, one of those people who span the world of the arts and sciences as well as the gap between the life of the Indian and the life of modern America."

Ella left behind many unpublished stories and manuscripts that are stored in various archives. Her *Dakota Family Life* manuscript was finally published in 2007 as *The Dakota Way of Life*. Sid Byrd, a Dakota man from Flandreau, South Dakota, said, "Ella Deloria has given us a precious gift of herself, her talents, and her intense desire for us to learn from our elders, which means embracing the Dakota way of life."

To honor Ella's work, in 2010 Columbia University created the Ella C. Deloria Undergraduate Research Fellowship. St. Mary's School in South Dakota offers a scholarship for a senior girl who carries on the Dakota way of life as shown in Ella's work.

Throughout her life, Ella Cara Deloria remained true to the vision that began with her grandfather, Saswe. Ella's hard work and sacrifices helped preserve the Dakota way of life. All this work was done, as she wrote in *Waterlily*, "so that my people may live!"

EXTEND YOUR LEARNING

The activities and additional information in the following pages are intended for use with the Charles Albert Bender, Ella Cara Deloria, and Peggy Flanagan books in the Minnesota Native Lives Series.

IDEAS FOR WRITING AND DISCUSSION

What Do You Think?

- What moment in this story do you think you will most remember? Why?

- Who do you believe was most important to this person's success? Why?

- What do you think were the hardest moments for this person? Why?

- How do you think this person was able to overcome hardship in their life?

- What were the happiest moments in the story of this person's life?

- What are some of the happiest moments in your life?

- What moment in the story reminded you of something in your own life?

- Write your own short autobiography, the story of your life so far, told by you!

IDEAS FOR VISUAL PROJECTS

Show Us What You Think

- Draw images for three or four moments that are not illustrated in this book.

- Draw a sketch of this person and include items they liked.

- Find images from American Indian boarding schools from the time this book covers.

- Find historic images to share of activities the book mentions. Are they different now?

- Find historic images to share of the reservations or places the book mentions.

- Make a map of the eleven tribal nations within the boundaries of the state of Minnesota. Where are they located? What tribe lives there? What else did you learn?

- Give a visual presentation on how treaties formed the White Earth Reservation, homeland of both Charles Albert Bender amd Peggy Flanagan. Explore "Why Treaties Matter" for information.

- Create a bar graph or pie chart or other infographic on one of these topics:

    1. How many Native Americans live in urban areas of Minnesota? Which cities in Minnesota are home to the largest populations of Native Americans?

    2. Many Native American students attend school in Minnesota—you may be one of them. How many Native American students are in your school district? How many tribes are represented?

Resources

- Minnesota Indian Education—Teaching and Learning: www.education.mn.gov/MDE/dse/indian/teach

- Why Treaties Matter: www.treatiesmatter.org/exhibit/ wp-content/uploads/2017/09/Updated-Sovereign-Nations1.pdf

IDEAS FOR FURTHER LEARNING

Dakota and Ojibwe people continue to live in Minnesota and are part of all aspects of our society. While English is a shared language, many Dakota and Ojibwe people also study and speak their Indigenous languages called Dakota and Anishinaabemowin.

Find Out More

- Find unfamiliar words in this book and create a glossary or word list with their definitions.

- Create a timeline for this person's life. Add dates from the timeline on page 45.

- Learn how to count to ten in Dakota or Ojibwe.

- Look up Ojibwe or Dakota words for baseball or ball games such as lacrosse.

- Learn about Dakota and Ojibwe sports and activities, such as powwows.

- Make a list of four common traditions the Ojibwe and Dakota share.

Resources

- Ojibwe People's Dictionary: ojibwe.lib.umn.edu

- Beginning Dakota: www.beginningdakota.org

- In Honor of the People: www.inhonorofthepeople.org

- Minnesota Historical Society, Minnesota Territory: www.mnhs.org/talesoftheterritory

- Ojibwe Material Culture: www.mnhs.org/ojibwematerialculture

- Oceti Sakowiŋ, The Seven Council Fires: www.mnhs.org/sevencouncilfires

Historical Context

Dakota and Ojibwe people live in today's context of the twenty-first century. We also have histories as rich and full of struggle as the US or other countries. This timeline presents important events in one place as a reminder that no one human history is more important than another, but history often makes it look that way. This timeline also provides context from Dakota and Ojibwe history. You can use it to respond to the books in this series by comparing each person's timeline and history to the events listed here.

Beyond memory, this place called Mni Sota Makoce, or Minnesota, is where the people became Dakota. They traveled as far north as Hudson Bay, as far west as the Rocky Mountains, south to trade with the Pueblos, and past the trading city of Cahokia, to the southeastern part of what later became the United States.

During this same time, Anishinaabeg, the larger group that includes Ojibwe people, lived far to the east of Minnesota, near the Atlantic Ocean. A series of prophecies, or visions of their future, set the Ojibwe off on their five-hundred-year journey to find a new home in "a land where food grows on water" (meaning manoomin, wild rice) along the Great Lakes and eventually in Minnesota.

TIMELINE

900	Dakota live, as they have always, in what will become Minnesota; ancestors of the Ojibwe begin migrating west to find a new homeland that was foretold in a vision.
1400	Ancestors of the Ojibwe reach the northwestern area of what later becomes Minnesota.
1540s	Spanish explorers map the Mississippi River and Dakota village sites.
1622	Ojibwe make contact with French explorer Étienne Brûlé at Lake Superior.
1689	Ojibwe fight for the French against the British until 1763 in what is now the US and Canada.
1730s	Ojibwe and Dakota begin battles over Dakota territories that end in the 1850s.
1769	Dartmouth College is founded to educate Native Americans in Christian theology.
1783	The American Revolution ends.
1805	Zebulon Pike and Dakota sign an agreement to sell land to the Americans in present-day Minneapolis. The Dakota are never paid for the land.

1812	Ojibwe and Dakota fight on the side of the British in the War of 1812.
1816	Saswe, Ella Cara Deloria's grandfather, is born in what is now Minnesota.
1819	Americans build a fort at Bdote (where the rivers meet in present-day St. Paul).
1825	Dakota and Ojibwe leaders and other tribes sign the Prairie du Chien Treaty and lose their land.
1830	Congress passes the Indian Removal Act. All Native Americans are required to move west of the Mississippi River. Many tribes remain in their homelands. Some are marched by force hundreds of miles from their homelands.
1837	A series of treaties begins where both Dakota and Ojibwe peoples' lands are taken away and many are forced to move.
1849	Minnesota Territory begins a period of organization (claiming) by the US that lasts until 1858.
1850s	Treaties require Dakota and Ojibwe to let go of hundreds of millions of acres of land.
1853	The 1851 treaties are ratified; American settlers encroach on Dakota lands.
1858	Minnesota becomes a state.
1858	Pay shah de o quay/Mary Razor, mother of Charles Albert Bender, is born.
1861	The American Civil War begins.

1862	War between the Dakota and the US begins in August. The fighting lasts six weeks.
1862	The Dakota ask the Ojibwe to protect their big drum during the war with the US.
1863	Treaties with Dakota people are repealed and almost all Dakota are removed from Minnesota.
1865	The American Civil War ends.
1867	The White Earth Reservation is established.
1870	Dakota and Ojibwe sign a peace treaty that remains unbroken.
1879	Colonel Richard Pratt founds the Carlisle Indian Boarding School.
1880s	Dakota people return to their communities in Minnesota.
1884	Charles Albert Bender is born in Brainerd, Minnesota.
1884	The Haskell Institute opens as a boarding school for Native American children.
1889	Ella Cara Deloria is born on the Yankton Reservation in South Dakota.
1902	Charles Albert Bender graduates from the Carlisle Indian School in Pennsylvania.
1914	Ella Cara Deloria graduates from Columbia University with a bachelor's degree in education.
1924	The Indian Citizenship Act of Congress grants citizenship to all Native Americans.

1925   Charles Albert Bender retires from professional baseball.

1932   Ella Cara Deloria publishes *Dakota Texts*.

1934   The Indian Reorganization Act is passed, forcing tribes to all operate by the same government model.

1944   Ella Cara Deloria publishes *Speaking of Indians*.

1953   Charles Albert Bender is inducted into the National Baseball Hall of Fame.

1953   The Termination Resolution by Congress is passed, intending to end US recognition of tribes.

1954   Charles Albert Bender dies in Pennsylvania.

1956   The Indian Relocation Act is passed to move Native Americans off reservations and into cities.

1971   Ella Cara Deloria dies in South Dakota.

1978   The Religious Freedom Act is passed, ending laws against religious and cultural practices of tribes.

1979   Peggy Flanagan is born in St. Louis Park, Minnesota.

1988   Ella Cara Deloria's *Waterlily* is published.

2007   Ella Cara Deloria's *The Dakota Way of Life* is published.

2019   Peggy Flanagan is sworn in as lieutenant governor of Minnesota, making her the highest-ranking Native American woman elected to an executive office in the United States.

ABOUT THE AUTHOR

Diane Wilson is a Dakota writer who uses personal experience to illustrate broader social and historical context. Her new novel, *The Seed Keeper*, will be published by Milkweed Editions in spring 2021. Her memoir *Spirit Car: Journey to a Dakota Past* won a 2006 Minnesota Book Award and was selected for the 2012 One Minneapolis One Read program. Her nonfiction book *Beloved Child: A Dakota Way of Life* was awarded the 2012 Barbara Sudler Award from History Colorado. Her work has been featured in many publications, including the anthology *A Good Time for the Truth*. She has served as a mentor for the Loft Emerging Artist program as well as Intermedia's Beyond the Pale. Awards she has received include the Minnesota State Arts Board, a 2013 Bush Foundation Fellowship, a 2018 AARP/Pollen 50 Over 50 Leadership Award, and the Jerome Foundation. She is a descendent of the Mdewakanton Oyate and enrolled on the Rosebud Reservation. Wilson currently serves as the executive director for the Native American Food Sovereignty Alliance.

ABOUT THE ILLUSTRATOR

Tashia Hart grew up in the wilds of Minnesota. She loves animals, writing, drawing, plants, and cooking. She is the author of *Gidjie and the Wolves* (Intermediaries, volume 1) and *Girl Unreserved* (Broken Wings and Things, volume 1). Her forthcoming wild rice cookbook, in partnership with the Minnesota Historical Society Press, is set to be released in the fall of 2021. She writes essays and recipes about wild foods for various organizations and tribal programs, and is an avid beader with thirty years of experience. She believes Indigenous people should control how their stories and likenesses are portrayed, and so has recently started the independent publishing company (Not) Too Far Removed Press. The mission of the press is to uplift fellow Indigenous authors and artists of the Midwest region. Tashia is Red Lake Anishinaabe. www.tashiahart.com

ABOUT THE SERIES EDITORS

Heid E. Erdrich is Ojibwe enrolled at the Turtle Mountain Reservation in North Dakota. She grew up in Wahpeton, North Dakota, not far from the White Earth Reservation in Minnesota and the Sisseton-Wahpeton Reservation in South Dakota. Her neighbors in her hometown were Dakota and Ojibwe from these tribal nations. Heid is the author of seven collections of poetry and a cookbook focused on indigenous foods of Minnesota and neighboring states titled *Original Local*. Her writing has won fellowships and awards from the National Poetry Series, Native Arts and Cultures Foundation, Minnesota State Arts Board, and more. She has twice won a Minnesota Book Award for poetry. A longtime teacher of writing at colleges and universities, Heid enjoys editing. She edited the anthologies *New Poets of Native Nations* from Graywolf Press, and *Sister Nations* from the Minnesota Historical Society Press. Heid's new poetry collection is *Little Big Bully*, Penguin Editions, 2020. Along with being Anishinaabe/Ojibwe, Heid's extended family includes Anishinaabe from several bands, Dakota, Hidatsa, Somali American, German American, and immigrants from India and elsewhere. She is also Metis, a group of people whose ancestors were French and Native American, and who lived in what became the United States and Canada. She loves the Great Lakes area and calls it home. Heid has lived in Minnesota for many years, raising her kids in Minneapolis, where they went to public schools. She enjoyed working with the authors and editors of this series of biographies and hopes you will read and reread these books!

Gwen Nell Westerman is Dakota and enrolled with the Sisseton Wahpeton Oyate in South Dakota. She is also a citizen of the Cherokee Nation. Her parents went to boarding schools in Oklahoma and South Dakota, and met at the Haskell Institute in Lawrence, Kansas. Gwen grew up in Oklahoma and Kansas among many different tribal nations. One of her earliest memories is when she was three, scribbling in a book. Her mother asked what she was doing and Gwen said, "I'm writing!" Today, she writes about Dakota history and language. She has won two Minnesota Book Awards for her work about Dakota people. Gwen's first poetry book was written in English and Dakota. Her poems have been published in anthologies, and so have her art quilts. Her quilt art received awards from the Minnesota State Arts Board, the Minnesota Historical Society, the Great Plains Art Museum, and the Heard Museum, and has been exhibited in many places across the United States. Her children were born in Oklahoma and grew up in Minnesota. Gwen's family tree includes teachers, leaders, and hard workers who were Dakota, Ojibwe, Odawa, and Cherokee, along with a few French and Scottish traders. She knows the names of all her ancestors on both sides of her family back before the American Revolution. She lives in Minnesota with her husband and their little black dog. She hopes you enjoy reading these books as much as she liked working on them, and that you will share them with your friends and families.